INTRODUCTION

What exactly is a Jack Russell Terrier? Who was Jack Russell, and why was a breed or strain of terrier named after him? These and many other questions about the Jack Russell aren't always easy to answer.

Terriers are generally small, working, earth dogs whose origins locale. Many types of terriers resulted, some of which have survived to this day; others have become extinct.

Originally intended for hunting and working, a new use was found for terriers in the 18th century in the blood sports of rat killing and badger baiting. Rat killing became

The Jack Russell Terrier is one of the best small game hunting dog breeds. JRs are alert and quick to catch their prey.

in England go back many centuries, even into the dark ages. The term "terrier" is taken from "terra," the Latin word for earth. The purpose of the dog was to "go to ground" in quest of game. As the modern nation we know as England evolved into its many regions, so too did the terrier. Regional strains of working terriers were developed to suit conditions and game in each a popular sport for the masses and the poor man's game or distraction. Given numbers of rats were placed in confined circles or squares. Competing terriers were then set upon them in turn. Each dog was timed. The dog that killed the rats in the shortest amount of time was the winner. Prizes went to the owners, and this soon became a great sport for the gambling public.

Jack Russell Terriers have the uncanny ability to sniff out and locate the holes of burrowing animals such as rats and badgers.

Winning dogs were highly prized and became valuable. Those with big reputations were in great demand as stud dogs. They themselves could command a small fortune when sold. Prize rat killers were

The English Bull Terrier was often bred to Jack Russells to make them tougher and more aggressive — to add a "killer instinct."

sometimes sent great distances to compete against other regional favorites.

Another sport that attracted the betting crowd in the 18th and well into the 19th century was badger baiting. A dog was sent down a badger hole or other hiding place to grab, pull or goad a badger out as many times as it could within a given time limit. The dog who got the badger out the most number of times was the winner.

Both of these sports required

In badger baiting, a popular sport in the 18th and 19th centuries, a JR was sent into a badger hole to grab, pull, or goad a badger out as many times as he could in a given time period.

terriers of exceptional strength and courage. The time-honored English regional terriers, used for ages as hunters and workers, needed some added toughness. This was accomplished by cross-breeding with the old English Bull Terrier and the Pit Bulldog. This blend produced a strain of mostly white sporting terriers, very tough and very brave, who were the ancestors of today's Jack Russell Terriers.

Jack Russells make excellent farm dogs. This JR has found a vantage point to look for the mice and rats that often inhabit barns and stables.

HISTORY OF THE JACK RUSSELL

The Jack Russell Terrier, or JR as he is often dubbed, was developed by an English country parson named Jack Russell who lived in Devonshire in the 19th century. Russell was no ordinary country parson. By all accounts, he was a flamboyant and swashbuckling man of the cloth who lived a very unconventional life. Russell was an avid sportsman. He is known to have maintained a large kennel of terriers throughout his adult life and is credited with developing terriers that were the forerunners of both the modern Jack Russell Terrier and the Wire-haired Fox Terrier.

Russell began collecting terriers and breeding them while still a divinity student at Oxford. One day while gazing out a school window, he caught a glimpse of a beautifully balanced white terrier perched on a milk wagon. Russell bought the dog on the spot. The white terrier, named Trump, became a legend in its own time and is thought to be the foundation bitch of the parson's line of working terriers.

Russell loved fox hunting and other field sports where man and dog worked in harmony. Consequently, he developed a passion for breeding fox hunting dogs. To this end, he bred Trump to his father's black and tan Devonshire Terrier (now extinct). Color, conformation, intelligence and character were bred with fox hunting in mind. The result was a balanced, compact, flexible body; straight legs; a small chest; and clean shoulders. This not only gave the Jack Russell Terriers speed for the chase, but it also gave them the ability to follow a fox down narrow tunnels in the earth. The classic JR philosophy was "where the fox can go, so must the terrier."

By the mid 1850s, Jack Russell was one of the best known breeders of fox terriers in southwestern England. Naturally, Russell's chief interest was in

Parson Jack Russell, who lived in Devonshire, England in the 19th century, was an avid collector of terriers and developed the breed named after him.

One of the distinguishing characteristics of the Jack Russell Terrier is that his coat is mostly white in color.

developing terriers that would only flush out a fox from its den or other hiding place to provide chasing sport for his hounds and fellow horse-borne hunters. We know Russell disapproved of breedings with bulldog bloodlines because terriers thus bred might be killers. Instead, Russell wanted terriers that would flush but not injure or kill the fox, which he considered most ungentlemanly. He also wanted to preserve the wild English fox for the fun of the chase, not to exterminate the species.

For that reason, Russell was careful to breed terriers without bulldog bloodlines. As stated, the accepted practice in the early 19th century and before had been to cross regional terriers with bulldogs and to introduce the bulldog strain into terrier breeding programs. This was done for the rat and badger competitions. Russell despised these so-called "sports," relegated to the lower classes of society and disdained by country gentry.

Russell's terriers have been variously described, but some characteristics are beyond dispute. They were small dogs of approximately 14 inches in height at the shoulder, 14 pounds, and mostly white in color. Some of his early terriers, purchased and brought in to breed into the line, were certainly some form of white-coated fox terriers that had gained popularity in the 18th century as useful fox hunters. There's no doubt they were the ancestor dogs of both the Jack Russell Terrier and the modern Fox Terrier.

The first JRs were long-legged for their size and generally had neither docked tails nor ears. Russell's first outstanding specimen was, of course, the bitch with a dot the size of a penny marking the tail. The coat was close and wiry and designed to protect the body from wet and cold. While this description matches that of the present day dog, this is where the

Various types of fox terriers were also bred into the line of JRs. These two wear an expression of excited anticipation. Did somebody say, "Rats"?

named Trump. According to legend, all JRs as we know them today are descended from this great terrier. Trump was described as a predominantly white dog with just a patch of dark tan over each eye and ear resemblance ends and legend and fact part company. The myth of a direct link between Trump and all JRs is just one of many controversies and schools of thought involving the JR. There are many others.

Used for fox hunting, the first JRs were long-legged for their size. Parson Jack Russell loved the hunt and bred his terriers for that purpose.

With a jaw grip like iron, the Jack Russell can hold on to quarry until his master pulls him out of the hole. This JR displays his grip on a low tree branch.

Due to his dislike of bulldog bloodlines, Russell was said to have preferred rough-coated terriers to smooth-coated ones because the smooth were more likely to have bulldog in their ancestry. Yet, this controversial parson had many smooth-coated terriers in his kennels and, according to eye witnesses and records of the time, these were bred into and were part of the original Jack Russell line. There is even controversy about Russell's motives and how they affected his activities as a breeder. Some critics argue that the evidence suggests that he was a dealer carelessly adding bloodlines without investigation to turn a quick profit, adding just about any terrier that appealed to him. The evidence for this view is the contrast between his modest income as a country parson and the large sums necessary to maintain his fox-hunting lifestyle

It is said that the Parson Jack Russell preferred the wirehaired type because the smoothhaired JRs were more likely to be aggressive due to their Bull Terrier ancestry.

and other gentlemanly pursuits. These critics claim that Russell bought, bred, traded and sold dogs to increase his income.

Whatever his motives, Russell's dogs were very popular, and dogs from his progeny were outcrossed into other terrier lines all throughout England in his lifetime. While there is no evidence of any direct genetic link or line of decent between today's JRs and the original stock owned by Russell, his influence on type and dimension is undeniable. While Russell never outcrossed with bulldogs or Bull Terriers, other breeders, including many who traded with Russell, were not so scrupulous. Besides occasional outcrosses with bulldogs, Beagle outcrossings were used at intervals by breeders all during the 19th century and added into the bloodlines of white working terriers. White-coated terriers with both smooth and rough coats became very popular. There was no strict uniformity or standard. Some were known as or called Jack Russell s, but most were simply called fox terriers.

There is a tenuous romantic link between today's JRs and those of the parson through the line of one Arthur Heineman, an equally legendary figure, reputed to be the last of the true Jack Russell breeders. Heineman died in 1933, and his dogs were sold off carelessly. Any dog claiming to be descended from the original JR stock can usually trace its ancestry back to Heineman's line, but the link, according to most experts, is very weak. The Heineman line was largely dissolved upon his death, and the thin line of descent that survived has been outcrossed so many times in the last 60 years that the line has been thinned to oblivion.

While the present-day Jack Russell Terrier is not directly related to the parson's dogs, and is at best a distant cousin or relation, it does resemble Russell's dogs in appearance. This is partly due to clever breeding and genetic engineering following the guidelines and descriptions handed down to us from contemporary accounts of the parson's dogs and their collateral relations. This attempt to recreate the "true" Jack Russell has given rise to a great controversy that has split the JR world into two opposing camps both in the US and the UK.

For a time, just about any small, white, working terrier of indeterminate origins that even remotely resembled the old Jack Russell standards, as described by Heineman and earlier commentators, were called Jack Russells. The modern JR, which falls into two distinct types, owes its revival to the formation of the Jack Russell Terrier Club of Great Britain in 1975. This club was founded by Mrs. Romayne Moore, the first patron of this remarkable renaissance. Earlier, Mrs. Moore had founded the Midland Working Terrier Club, which was devoted to promoting the working terrier group.

The Midland Working Terrier Club dissolved while Mrs. Moore was out of the country in the late

1960s. Upon her return, she organized the Jack Russell Terrier Club of Great Britain. The new club set up a standard that allowed any white, working terrier that conformed to a rough description of the JR to be registered. There was also an advanced register reserved for allegedly better dogs over 18 months of age. These dogs had to conform to a higher standard for height, legs, fronts and other descriptive standards. Inspectors were appointed to pass on the qualifications of candidates for the advanced register.

It was hoped that the advanced register would provide a nucleus for desired breedings, which would bring about a standard of excellence that would gain acceptance in the form of a consensus amongst owners and breeders. It didn't work out that way. The inspectors ended up applying varying standards, and the goal of achieving a top quality standard was not realized. Thus, while the object and intention of the founders of the club was to conform as closely as possible to the older descriptions, no fixed type evolved. Even during the parson's lifetime, white, working terriers with shorter legs and longer backs were popular throughout England. These dogs had their admirers and partisans among the inspectors, and many found their way into the advanced registry.

The years between the passing of the Heineman strain and the Moore renaissance are called the "lean years." During these so called "lean years," the Jack Russell Terrier was first brought to the US. Many were imported by Americans who had lived or visited in England and had fallen in love with the little, white dog. While the JR was a big hit with the horsy set, most of the JRs brought into the US were of the shorter-legged, longer-backed variety associated with badger baiting or ratting. These dogs were better suited to city and suburban living and were no doubt less active than their longer-legged cousins. Many of these dogs and many sold today as pure JRs are very different than the animal Parson Jack Russell had in mind and probably would have been taken out of his breeding program as undesirable.

Developments in England were fast paced and furious. The registry created even more controversy than it was originally supposed to cure. Fights, confrontations and arguments of great complexity resulted. Highly partisan groups of owners banded together against others. Size, weight, height and type of coat were all in dispute. One of the main contentions was over the two types or sizes: the long-legged, taller dog, conforming to the Heineman standard of 12–14 inches; and the short-legged, proportionally longer-backed dog of 9–12 inches, so popular in the US. By far, the greatest division came on the issue of recognition by the Kennel Club of Great Britain. Generally, the English Jack Russell Club had been opposed to recognition for fear that it would spoil the breed in the same way other breeds were altered to fit a false standard of conformation.

There was always an element within the JRC of Great Britain that favored recognition, if only to establish its legitimacy as a pure-bred dog. When this faction became bolder and more strident in their demands, a serious rift developed among the membership. The dissident group supporting recognition left the club and set up a rival organization — the Parson Jack Russell Terrier Club of Great Britain. In addition to recognition, this club favored a long-legged standard, claiming kinship to the original JR standard of old Parson Jack.

This, in turn, forced many partisans of the smaller, short-legged dog who were originally against recognition to change their position in favor of it for fear that the long-legged dog would become the only breed standard through kennel club validation. Formal recognition came in January, 1990. The JR Terrier was recognized by the KC of Great Britain as a variant of the Fox Terrier. Dogs in the registry of the Parson Jack Russell Terrier Club were accepted within generational parameters, as were their siblings. Thus in England, at least the longer-legged, more balanced dog was validated.

In the US, events kept pace. With the increasing popularity of the breed came the establishment of the Jack Russell Terrier Club of America in 1976 by Alisa

The proportionally longer backed Jack Russell Terrier standing 9–12 inches at the withers is very popular in the United States.

Beagle outcrossings were also used at intervals throughout the 19th century in the breeding of the Jack Russell Terrier.

Crawford of Maryland. The club sponsors hunts, obedience trials, field trials and other special events.

As with the earlier JRC of Great Britain, the JRC of America is adamantly opposed to formal registration of the breed by the AKC. The club is dedicated to maintaining the JR's hunting and working characteristics. To this day, grooming tables are forbidden at the JRTCA specialty shows.

An almost identical political situation evolved in the US. The JRTCA adopted the same variable standard as the JRC of Great Britain, finding a place within the standard for the shorter-legged, smaller, sometimes longer-backed, 10-inch dog. In a roundabout way, this led to the formation of what became a splinter group — the JR Breeder's Association. A very complex and turbulent set of developments eventually led to opposing positions nearly identical to the division in England. The Breeder's Association favored the long-legged, square dog as well as formal recognition and registration with the AKC. The split is bitter and seemingly irreconcilable. The Breeder's Association and the Parson group in England consider themselves purists, true to Parson Jack Russell's original breedings. Both sought recognition and registration to validate their positions. Conversely in the US, the JRTCA has disdained the AKC's recognition, as the JRC of Great Britain opposed the KC of Great Britain's recognition.

The JRBA made formal application for AKC registration in September, 1995. While their intention is to preserve the original type and standard of the old JR, the application creates a dilemma for the AKC. The larger, longer-legged, fleet-footed hunter of the Parson Jack Russell Terrier Club of Great Britain has been embraced and adopted by the Kennel Club of Great Britain. A similar standard, if adopted in the US, would invalidate the far more popular smaller dogs with shorter legs, the ones many JR lovers feel are more suited to American conditions, both hunting and domestic. Furthermore, many long-legged, square, nicely balanced, white terriers of between 10–12+ inches in height would also be invalidated. These smaller dogs fall beautifully within every breed standard, even that of the Parson Club in the UK and the Breeder's Association in the US, save for their size.

THE JACK RUSSELL TERRIER CLUB OF AMERICA

The Jack Russell Terrier Club of America, with over 6,000 members, is firmly committed to preserving the working abilities

The Jack Russell Terrier has been the source of much debate in England and the US—some want the larger, longer-legged dogs, and others want the short-legged, longer–backed dogs.

From England in the 1930s this is C.C. Walters, early JR breeder and fancier, with two of his JRs. Notice the Fox Terrier influence in these Walters JRs.

and associated characteristics of this great, little, fox-hunting dog. The club stresses function over form. To the JRTCA, the Jack Russell Terrier is merely an extension of the early, unspoiled 19th century Fox Terrier and is indeed the true Fox Terrier. To this end, the club has promoted a broad standard that ranges from 10–15 inches at the withers. To the JRTCA, a Jack Russell Terrier is a type or broad strain of working terrier rather than a pure breed. The standard is broad enough to include a variety of types and colors as well as variety in size. That is what the so-called "two types" are really all about — size.

This broad standard is a deliberate attempt to meet the working and hunting needs of its members. It really says, "we have heavily weighted the standard in favor of function over form. We did this so that both the big dogs with long legs bred for the fast chase and the smaller more compact dogs with short legs bred for flushing out small game in holes are within the standard." As long as they meet the minimal conformation norm for their size, they are classified as Jack Russell Terriers. In other words, it says, "Hang the old parson!" If a white working terrier meets the earlier described requirements and meets the design standard hammered out over the years for the hunting function it is to perform, it is a Jack Russell Terrier — old Jack or no old Jack.

In fairness, it would be wrong to associate the JRTCA with short-

Even at the water's edge, the Jack Russell attempts to follow its quarry, but it looks like this time it got away.

Jack Russell breeders are dedicated to keeping the Jack Russell Terrier a working and hunting dog by stressing function over form.

legged, long-backed terriers and the Breeder's Association with long-legged, square dogs. The JRTCA standard, while broad and accepting of variety, is also very specific on many points. The description for the club's breed standard describes the JR as "a sturdy, tough terrier, very much on its toes all the time, measuring between 10 and 15 inches at the withers. The body length must be in proportion to the height, and it should present a compact, balanced image, always being in solid, hard condition." There are similar specifications for head, eyes, ears, mouth, body, fore and hindquarters, feet, tail, coat, color and gait.

The Parson Jack Russell Club in England has successfully achieved recognition for a narrow portion of the breed standard in England. The Breeder's Association is attempting to do the same thing in the US. Their rationale is that they are the purists recreating Parson Jack's own dogs exactly to his taste. This contradicts the philosophy of the JR clubs of America and Great Britain. They feel, with considerable justification, that historical evidence varies and is subject to interpretation, which suggests that a wider variety of white, working fox terriers qualify in every sense as JRs.

In fairness to the Breeder's Association and the Parson's Club, members are not trying to "fancy" the breed. They are trying to achieve world-wide recognition of the dog as a pure breed and to validate their purist view of the standard. An ironic and strong endorsement for the JRTCA's philosophy is the fact that Parson Jack Russell was himself a founder of the Kennel Club of Great Britain and was a judge at some of its early shows. None of his own dogs were ever exhibited, and he made no attempt to achieve recognition or registration for them from the club.

In Britain, it should be noted, the type of quarry hunted is very different than in the US, where it tends to be smaller in size. American JRs are used to hunt a variety of game, including the smaller American fox, raccoon, woodchuck and badger. This made the smaller JRs very popular in the US and supports the JRTCA's position. Some JRTCA members claim with some amusement that English judges at American shows tend to favor larger JRs, not just in conformation, but in field and work trials as well.

The JRTCA holds shows that reward conformation within the standard but also emphasize the hunting and field qualities of the breed. Only dogs that conform to the standard are listed in the JRTCA registry. Dogs with congenital defects are ineligible, unlike other dogs registered with the AKC.

Grooming, while encouraged, is not paramount and is not a factor or consideration in trials. Indeed, there has been an increase in conformation showing in recent years at Jack Russell breed shows. This is tolerated as a means of promoting correct conformation to the breed standard that stresses the hardy, tough, hunting character of the breed. The highest JRTCA awards go to field and work trial winners, not to dogs groomed to show well as a matter of form.

These JRs dig and sniff around hoping to get the scent of some small game. JRs are always ready for the hunt.

The Jack Russell Terrier is described as "a sturdy, tough terrier, very much on its toes all the time."

BREED STANDARD

For showing purposes, terriers are classified into two groups: 10" to 12"; and over 12" and up to 15".

Old scars or injuries, the result of work or accident, should not be allowed to prejudice a terrier's chance in the show ring unless they interfere with its movement or with its utility for work or stud. The following is the Jack Russell Terrier Club of America's breed standard.

CHARACTERISTICS

The Terrier must present a lively, active and alert appearance. It should impress with its fearless and happy disposition. It should be remembered that the Jack Russell is a working terrier and should retain these instincts. Nervousness, cowardice or over-aggressiveness should be discouraged, and it should always appear confident.

GENERAL APPEARANCE

A sturdy, tough terrier, very much on its toes all the time, measuring between 10" and 15" at the withers. The body length must be in proportion to the height, and it should present a compact, balanced image, always being in solid, hard condition.

The head of the JR should be well balanced and in proportion to the body with moderately thick, small, "V" shaped ears carried forward.

HEAD

Should be well balanced and in proportion to the body. The skull should be flat, of moderate width at the ears, narrowing to the eyes. There should be a defined stop but not over pronounced. The length of muzzle from the nose to the stop should be slightly shorter than the distance from the stop to the occiput. The nose should be black. The jaw should be powerful and well boned with strongly muscled cheeks.

EYES

Should be almond shaped, dark in color and full of life and intelligence.

EARS

Small "V" shaped drop ears carried forward close to the head and of moderate thickness.

MOUTH

Strong teeth with the top slightly overlapping the lower.

(Note: a level bite is acceptable for registration.)

NECK
Clean and muscular, of good length, gradually widening at the shoulders.

FOREQUARTERS
The shoulders should be sloping and well laid back, fine at points and clearly cut at the withers. Forelegs should be strong and straight bones with joints in correct alignment. Elbows hanging perpendicular to the body and working free of the sides.

BODY
The chest should be shallow, narrow and the front legs set not too widely apart, giving an athletic, rather than heavily chested appearance. As a guide only, the chest should be small enough to be easily spanned behind the shoulders, by average sized hands, when the terrier is in a fit, working condition. The back should be strong, straight and, in comparison to the height of the terrier, give a balanced image. The loin should be slightly arched.

HINDQUARTERS
Should be strong and muscular, well put together with good angulation and bend of stifle, giving plenty of drive and propulsion. Looking from behind, the hocks must be straight.

FEET
Round, hard padded, of cat-like appearance, neither turning in nor out.

TAIL
Should be set rather high,

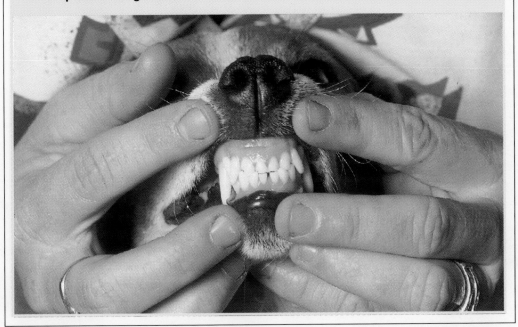

A Jack Russell Terrier's top teeth should slightly overlap his lower teeth, but a level bite is acceptable for registration.

carried gaily and in proportion to the body length, usually about four inches long, providing a good hand-hold.

COAT

Smooth, without being so sparse as not to provide a certain amount of protection from the elements and undergrowth. Rough or broken coated, without being woolly.

COLOR

White should predominate (i.e., must be more than 51% white) with tan, black, or brown markings. Brindle markings are unacceptable.

GAIT

Movement should be free, lively, well coordinated with straight action in front and behind.

Male animals should have two testicles fully descended into the scrotum.

A Jack Russell Terrier should not show any strong characteristics of another breed.

FAULTS

Shyness. Disinterest. Overly aggressive. Defects in bite. Weak jaws. Fleshy ears. Down at shoulder. Barrel ribs. Out at elbow. Narrow hips. Straight stifles. Weak feet. Sluggish or unsound movement. Dishing. Plaiting. Toeing. Silky or woolly coats. Too much color (less than 51% white). Shrill or weak voice. lack of muscle or skin tone. Lack of stamina or lung reserve. Evidence of foreign blood.

A straight back helps to give the strength and balance necessary to drag quarry from its hole, but in case the dog can't, a 4-inch long tail provides a good hand-hold for the owner to pull the dog out.

The eyes of a Jack Russell are dark, almond shaped, and full of life and intelligence.

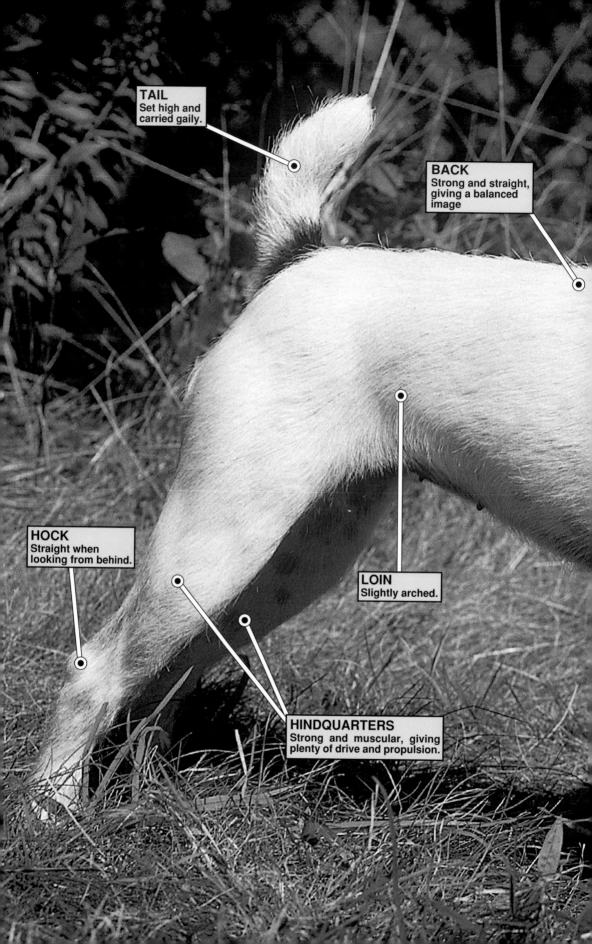

TAIL
Set high and carried gaily.

BACK
Strong and straight, giving a balanced image

HOCK
Straight when looking from behind.

LOIN
Slightly arched.

HINDQUARTERS
Strong and muscular, giving plenty of drive and propulsion.

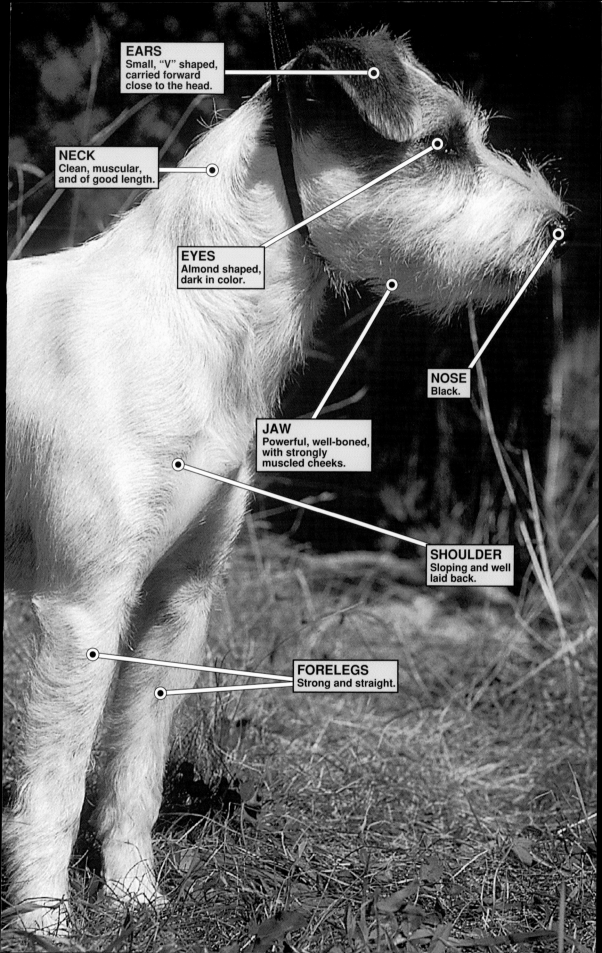

EARS
Small, "V" shaped, carried forward close to the head.

NECK
Clean, muscular, and of good length.

EYES
Almond shaped, dark in color.

NOSE
Black.

JAW
Powerful, well-boned, with strongly muscled cheeks.

SHOULDER
Sloping and well laid back.

FORELEGS
Strong and straight.

DESCRIPTION

The Jack Russell Terrier is a dog whose hunting qualities have been lovingly preserved through the ages. As with any hunting breed, the JR has strong natural instincts that need an outlet. Exercise is of paramount importance. The more room he has to run the better. Despite his

One of the reasons the shorter-legged, longer-backed JR is so popular in the US is precisely because of its adaptability to cramped space.

Nonetheless, prospective owners must remember that first and foremost, the JR is a hunting dog. Even the most domesticated

Jack Russell Terriers love to chase and need lots of attention, so make sure that you have lots of safe toys and the time to play with your JR.

small size, the JR is not a lap dog. In fact, keeping JRs as house pets is a relatively recent development and a great departure from their usual lifestyle. With proper training, the JR can easily adapt and become a member of the household. It also makes a wonderful companion dog. But the JR can also adapt to city life under the right circumstances.

animal will do much better if it is run every day and given lots of sport. Running after objects around the house, chasing balls up and down stairs, and romps around the couch will help if you don't have a large fenced-in area or can't take your JR to a field or similar surrounding.

While the JR is very trainable and makes a great companion, its basic instinct can create special problems for owners. No matter how highly trained and responsive your dog may be, the training can be overcome at any moment by a powerful stimulus like a squirrel, bird or even a motor vehicle. For this reason, don't ever allow your JR to run in open, public places. If you don't have a fenced-in yard, the dog should be exercised on a long (100—150 foot) lead, which when fully extended will keep your JR out of harm's way.

Homeowners taking on the responsibility of a JR are well advised to fence in their yards with at least a four-foot chain-link fence. A stockade fence of 6 feet or more is preferable. There are cases, albeit rare, of JRs climbing their way out of a chain-link fence paw by paw. If you find you have such a clever and agile pet, an angled return can be added at the top of a chain-link fence to

Remember that first and foremost the Jack Russell is a hunting dog, and at any moment he might jump up and chase a moving object or animal.

The Jack Russell is not a lap dog! JRs need plenty of exercise, and the more room the better.

JRs are natural diggers and have been known to dig for quarry and disappear for days in underground holes and tunnels when off their leads.

discourage even the most athletic of JRs. Invisible fencing may also provide good results.

However, even the highest fence does not eliminate the need for firm discipline. The hunting instinct is so strongly imprinted into the JR's genes, that the dog has an aggressive nature. The JR is prone to chase cars, motorcycles, bicycles, golf carts, and all kinds of moving vehicles, even vacuum cleaners! Digging also comes very naturally to the breed. A JR off the lead has been known to disappear underground following holes and tunnels made by groundhogs, raccoons, and other animals that tunnel into the earth. This can result in tragic consequences for the unknowing and/or baffled owner who can't seem to find his dog. JRs have been known to stay underground hanging onto quarry for days at a time. One of the reasons for the breed standard regarding the length of the tail was to give the owner a means of grabbing the dog from behind and pulling it out of the hole it was working.

The JR owner must always remember that this feisty little terrier was bred to go underground and grab quarry for the purpose of pulling, dragging, and/or flushing it out. Many of the short-legged and longer-backed JRs kept as pets cannot adequately perform this function. They don't have enough reach or balance, nor do they have enough neck or upper body strength to follow quarry to ground and perform the necessary clutch and grab function. While these dogs may not qualify for registry and may be considered "not functional" by JR authorities, they still have the same digging ability and aggressive instincts, so be vigilant.

A Jack Russell could easily dig his way under poor fencing. Fortunately there is no dirt for this JR to dig, but be sure to erect proper fencing to avoid any problems.

YOUR NEW JACK RUSSELL PUPPY

SELECTION

When you do pick out a Jack Russell puppy as a pet, don't be hasty; the longer you study puppies, the better you will understand them. Make it your transcendent concern to select only one that radiates good health and spirit and is lively on his feet, whose eyes are bright, whose coat shines, and who comes forward eagerly to make and to cultivate your acquaintance. Don't fall for any shy little darling that wants to retreat to his bed or his box, or plays coy behind other puppies or people, or hides his head under your arm or jacket appealing to your protective instinct. *Pick the Jack Russell puppy who forthrightly picks you! The feeling of attraction should be mutual!*

There should be a mutual feeling of attraction between you and the Jack Russell puppy you choose to be your companion.

DOCUMENTS

Now, a little paper work is in order. When you purchase a purebred Jack Russell puppy, you should receive a transfer of ownership, registration material, and other "papers" (a list of the immunization shots, if any, the puppy may have been given; a note on whether or not the puppy has been wormed; a diet and feeding schedule to which the puppy is accustomed) and you are welcomed as a fellow owner to a long, pleasant association with a most lovable pet, and more (news)paper work.

GENERAL PREPARATION

You have chosen to own a particular Jack Russell puppy. You have chosen it very carefully over all other breeds and all other puppies. So before you ever get that Jack Russell puppy home, you will have prepared for its arrival by reading everything you can get your hands on having to do with the management of Jack Russells and puppies. True, you will run into many conflicting

JRs are popular with horse trainers and breeders. This little rodeo doll is owned by Barbara Dady.

Wrapped in a towel and carried in the arms or lap of a passenger, the Jack Russell puppy will usually make the trip without mishap. If the pup starts to drool and to squirm, stop the car for a few minutes. Have newspapers handy in case of car-sickness. A covered carton lined with newspapers provides protection for puppy and car, if you are driving alone. Avoid excitement and unnecessary handling of the puppy on arrival. A Jack Russell puppy is a very small "package" to be making a complete change of surroundings and company, and he needs frequent rest and refreshment to renew his vitality.

THE FIRST DAY AND NIGHT

When your Jack Russell puppy arrives in your home, put him

opinions, but at least you will not be starting "blind." Read, study, digest. Talk over your plans with your veterinarian, other "Jack Russell people," and the seller of your Jack Russell puppy.

When you get your Jack Russell puppy, you will find that your reading and study are far from finished. You've just scratched the surface in your plan to provide the greatest possible comfort and health for your Jack Russell; and, by the same token, you do want to assure yourself of the greatest possible enjoyment of this wonderful creature. You must be ready for this puppy mentally as well as in the physical requirements.

TRANSPORTATION

If you take the puppy home by car, protect him from drafts, particularly in cold weather.

If you are going by car on the way home from the seller, your new JR puppy should be wrapped in a towel and kept on a passenger's lap to keep him warm and safe.

down on the floor and don't pick him up again, except when it is absolutely necessary. He is a dog, a real dog, and must not be lugged around like a rag doll. Handle him as little as possible, and permit no one to pick him up and baby him. To repeat, *put your Jack Russell puppy on the floor or the ground and let him stay there except when it may be necessary to do otherwise.*

Quite possibly your Jack Russell puppy will be afraid for a while in his new surroundings, without his mother and littermates. Comfort him and reassure him, but don't console him. Don't give him the "oh-you-poor-itsy-bitsy-puppy" treatment. Be calm, friendly, and reassuring. Encourage him to walk around and sniff over his new home. If it's dark, put on the lights. Let him roam for a few minutes while you and everyone else concerned sit

quietly or go about your routine business. Let the puppy come back to you.

Playmates may cause an immediate problem if the new Jack Russell puppy is to be greeted by children or other pets. If not, you can skip this subject. The natural affinity between puppies and children calls for some supervision until a live-and-let-live relationship is established. This applies particularly to a Christmas puppy, when there is more excitement than usual and more chance for a puppy to swallow something upsetting. It is a better plan to welcome the puppy several days before or after the holiday week. Like a baby, your Jack Russell puppy needs much rest and should not be over-handled. Once a child realizes that a puppy has "feelings" similar to his own, and can readily be hurt or injured, the

The Christmas JR can present a particularly bad situation, as the holiday hustle and bustle can be overwhelming for a small puppy. It is best to wait for the excitement of Christmas to be over before bringing a puppy into the home.

No matter how much your JR puppy cries or begs to be picked up, it is best not to give in. He needs to get used to his new environment, and too much handling will spoil him.

opportunities for play and responsibilities provide exercise and training for both.

For his first night with you, he should be put where he is to sleep every night—say in the kitchen, since its floor can usually be easily cleaned. Let him explore the kitchen to his heart's content; close doors to confine him there. Prepare his food and feed him lightly the first night. Give him a pan with some water in it—not a lot, since most puppies will try to drink the whole pan dry. Give him an old coat or shirt to lie on. Since a coat or shirt will be strong in human scent, he will pick it out to lie on, thus furthering his feeling of security in the room where he has just been fed.

HOUSEBREAKING HELPS

Now, sooner or later—mostly sooner—your new Jack Russell puppy is going to "puddle" on the floor. First take a newspaper and lay it on the puddle until the urine is soaked up onto the paper. *Save this paper.* Now take a cloth with soap and water, wipe up the floor and dry it well. Then take the wet paper and place it on a fairly large square of newspapers in a convenient corner. When cleaning up, always keep a piece of wet paper on top of the others. Every time he wants to "squat," he will seek out this spot and use the papers. (This routine is rarely necessary for more than three days.) Now leave your Jack Russell puppy for the night. Quite probably he will cry and howl a bit; some are more stubborn than others on this matter. But let him stay alone for the night. This may seem harsh treatment, but it is the best procedure in the long run. Just let him cry; he will weary of it sooner or later.

Properly socialized JR puppies should have minimal problems entering a home with other pets, Even so, introductions should be careful and gradual.

OWNING A JACK RUSSELL

The human master must exert firm, intelligent, well-balanced discipline to own a JR, and for that reason, the dog is not for everyone. People incapable of providing proper discipline because of disposition or other circumstances, should not own a JR. Although JRs are loving, the children appear well-disciplined. They reason that if parents are incapable of controlling their children, they can hardly be expected to control a JR.

An untrained, unsupervised JR will, in the words of one noted breeder, "self-destruct."

Always poised and ready to pounce, a Jack Russell Terrier needs firm discipline and lots of intense exercise to keep him happy and well-adjusted.

intelligent companion animals, they are not necessarily good with children. The JR will not tolerate the torture and abuse often inflicted on an animal by young children. Hair, tail or ear pulling will not be endured for long without a response. There are many breeders who will not sell a JR to any household with children under six years of age. Other breeders will only sell a dog to a home with children if The dog will be restless, irritable and nervous. JRs are best behaved and most well-adjusted when they are worked, run and exercised intensively. This, along with proper discipline, will result in a happy, loving, well-adjusted pet that will provide many years of loyal and devoted companionship. JRs are also very protective and quick to defend their human family and property from real or imagined dangers.

Parson Jack Russell loved the hunt and chase but was firmly against killing, so he bred JRs to flush out game but not to kill it. These JRs bolt into a haystack following their quarry.

Constantly on the move, JRs have a high energy and activity level. Will you be able to keep up with a JR if you decide to have one as a pet?

NATURE OF THE JR

The JR is not a killer by nature; it was not bred to kill. Parson Jack Russell himself loved the hunt and the chase with the exciting flushing of the quarry and the physically enduring pursuit over hill and dale. He was, however, firmly against killing. Other regional terriers like the Lakeland are bred to locate quarry and then go in and kill it. Conversely, the JR goes in and bays, holds onto, and keeps the game busy until the terrier man catches up, pulls the dog out, and releases the game for the chase. The JR is also used to flush out game. Knowledge of this special characteristic that distinguishes JRs from other working terriers can be useful in the care and training of a JR.

Two Jack Russell Terriers are good exercise for each other. These frisky pups splash around with each other in the water.

It is very important to understand the special nature of this terrier and why the breed exists at all. Lacking this understanding, the owner would find the JR's behavior perplexing. The training of any animal must take into account its natural propensities, or it is doomed to failure. At first glance, the JR is a cute, compact, little dog. Such lack of knowledge and understanding of the breed has resulted in many unwanted and abandoned JRs. Sadly, most of these dogs are unwanted for doing what comes natural. An initial investigation before purchasing a dog can prevent this from happening. New owners sometimes find themselves unprepared to give the kind of care the JR requires.

Ignorance of the dog's hunting instinct and high activity level often produces a mismatch between pet and owner. This has become more commonplace in recent years with the increasing popularity of the breed in the US. The JR's status as a "rare breed" has given it an added exotic allure and has made it desirable to many potential owners. Many of these people live in urban or suburban settings and are unable to provide the proper environment for the dog. Working owners are sometimes out all day and unable to give the dog the daily time and attention it needs. Apartment dwellers are frequently incapable of maintaining the high level of physical activity the JR requires. In some cases, indifferent discipline, training and lack of interest cause the JR to become unruly and unmanageable.

When it comes to swimming, JRs are very adept. However, make sure you supervise your dog so that an accident cannot occur.

Jack Russell Terriers *do* enjoy a relaxing nap in the sun sometimes—after all, it's hard to be active all the time!

Chewed carpets, furniture and articles of clothing may become the legacy of such a situation.

It is always useful and productive if there is a strong Alpha presence in the home. In happy JR households, frequently one family member assumes a dominant role over the dog.

JR RESCUE

The JRTCA maintains a rescue service for dogs who are unwanted or abandoned because they didn't fit in with their previous owners lifestyle or temperament. The Russell Rescue, as it is called, is a network of JRTCA members dedicated to finding good homes for these unwanted animals. As with other breeds, the rescue organization acts as a half-way house between original and prospective owners. Care is given in selecting suitable new homes for these animals that might otherwise end up in shelters or loose on the streets. Responsibilities, including spaying and neutering, are placed on the original owners when possible. Financial requirements for crates and re-location expenses are placed on adoptive owners.

The Russell Rescue maintains a list of available foster homes designed to provide temporary shelter during the transitional stage. The network exists and operates mostly on private donations. It s members are devoted to saving as many JRs as possible as well as trying to prevent situations that create unwanted JRs. To this end, they do their best to educate buyers and to persuade breeders never to sell or give a puppy to anyone who is not knowledgeable about the needs and characteristics of the breed.

Many Jack Russells become abandoned by owners who can't keep up with the active lifestyle of their dogs. This woman, however, enjoys her two playful pups.

TEMPERAMENT

The JR has an aggressive nature that makes it absolutely fearless. It won't hesitate to tackle quarry much larger than itself and will attack and tangle with much larger dogs, if provoked. For this reason, it is never a good idea, although there are exceptions, to leave two or more JRs of the same sex alone and unattended for more than very short intervals. Because the JR is still a natural breed, the pack instinct is very strong. These pack oriented little dogs are very quick to establish a hierarchy, or pecking order, with dominant dogs emerging as leaders. There is always the danger of a challenge for position between two or more dogs, with serious fights resulting. There are documented cases of killings, even when there are only two dogs. When there are several dogs together, there is the added risk that the group will attack and destroy a fallen or severely injured dog. This is also well-documented. Female JRs can be dangerous to other females when they are in heat or pregnant. Females should never be left unattended during those times. The same holds true when JRs are in mixed company with other breeds.

Sometimes JRs adapt well to

Not all JRs get along. Many times, because they are so in tune with their natural instincts, same-sex JRs need to establish a hierarchy—they need a pack leader.

Although most Jack Russells do not accept other small pets, such as ferrets, hamsters, and birds, this JR plays happily with the family cat.

other dogs in the house. This is more likely to happen if the other dog is of the opposite sex. There are many reports of JRs adjusting well to dogs of the same sex, providing the other dog has a good temperament and a competitive situation does not develop. JR owners should get to know their dogs very well before introducing another dog into the household. A knowledge of the dog's breeding line and genetic strain will help, but even with the best information and experience, surprises are always possible.

As a rule, JRs do not do well with other pets. There is always a real danger that a JR will harass and kill smaller pets like ferrets, hamsters, birds and other small game. JRs sometimes tolerate cats, but will not be intimidated by feline spitting, clawing or arching of the back. With some exceptions, it isn't a good idea to mix JRs with cats because cats often fall prey to the dog's aggressive nature, which leads to tragic results.

JRs make good farm dogs because they have a natural protective instinct and are not afraid to tangle with much larger animals.

GROOMING YOUR JACK RUSSELL

JRs are divided into coat types. There are three coat types: smooth, rough and broken. Many JR owners are surprised to learn that their short-haired, smooth-coated dogs shed lots of white hairs. This could present a problem for people with allergies and respiratory ailments. Short-more comfortable in warmer weather. Combing in confined spaces with limited ventilation can also be a problem for allergy sufferers.

Grooming for form's sake, rather than for health or function, is far less important for the JR than it is for other breeds.

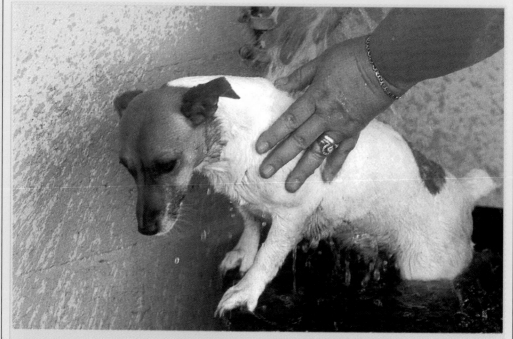

Because Jack Russells are earth dogs and like to dig as often as they can, you may find that your JR needs to be bathed frequently.

haired JRs can leave a trail of hairs on rugs, furniture, car mats and woolens of all types.

Rough and broken-coated JRs shed much less. They develop a heavier undercoat than the smooth-haired dog. The undercoat should be combed often to remove dead hair. Combing will not only make your JR look better, it will also make it Because it is a hunting dog, the JR needs special attention paid to its ears and eyes. There are several eye and ear cleaners sold over-the-counter that you can use to keep your JR's ears and eyes free from dirt and irritation. If you are unsure of what to use, ask your veterinarian to prescribe something.

Because they are hunting dogs, JRs come in contact with irritants, both underground and in the water, that can affect their ears and eyes. Therefore special attention must be paid to these parts during grooming.

FEEDING YOUR JACK RUSSELL

Now let's talk about feeding your Jack Russell, a subject so simple that it's amazing there is so much nonsense and misunderstanding about it. Is it expensive to feed a Jack Russell? No, it is not! You can feed your Jack Russell economically and keep him in perfect shape the year round, or you can feed him expensively. He'll thrive either way, and let's see why this is true.

First of all, remember a Jack Russell is a dog. Dogs do not have a high degree of selectivity in their food, and unless you spoil them with great variety (and possibly turn them into poor, "picky" eaters) they will eat almost anything that they become accustomed to.

Fresh cool water should always be made available to your Jack Russell Terrier, especially in hot weather when there is danger of dehydration or becoming overheated.

Many dogs flatly refuse to eat nice, fresh beef. They pick around it and eat everything else. But meat—bah! Why? They aren't accustomed to it! They'd eat rabbit fast enough, but they refuse beef because they aren't used to it.

VARIETY NOT NECESSARY

A good general rule of thumb is forget all human preferences and don't give a thought to variety. Choose the right diet for your Jack Russell and feed it to him day after day, year after year, winter and summer. But what is the right diet?

Hundreds of thousands of dollars have been spent in canine nutrition research. The results are pretty conclusive, so you needn't go into a lot of experimenting with trials of this and that every other week. Research has proven just what your dog needs to eat and to keep healthy.

DOG FOOD

There are almost as many right diets as there are dog experts, but the basic diet most often recommended is one that consists of a dry food, either meal or kibble form. There are several of excellent quality, manufactured by reliable companies, research tested, and nationally advertised. They are inexpensive, highly

Feeding your Jack Russell a consistent diet day after day is the best way to keep him healthy. Variety may make your dog a picky eater.

don't worry about carbohydrate and mineral levels. These substances are plentiful and cheap and not likely to be lacking in a good brand.

The advice given for how to choose a dry food also applies to moist or canned types of dog foods, if you decide to feed one of these.

Having chosen a really good food, feed it to your Jack Russell as the manufacturer directs. And once you've started, stick to it. Never change if you can possibly help it. A switch from one meal or kibble-type food can usually be made without too much upset;

Treats are fine occasionally, but too many treats in addition to his regular meals can upset the balance of your JR's diet.

satisfactory, and easily available in stores everywhere in containers of five to 50 pounds. Larger amounts cost less per pound, usually.

If you have a choice of brands, it is usually safer to choose the better known one; but even so, carefully read the analysis on the package. Do not choose any food in which the protein level is less than 25 percent, and be sure that this protein comes from both animal and vegetable sources. The good dog foods have meat meal, fish meal, liver, and such, plus protein from alfalfa and soy beans, as well as some dried-milk product. Note the vitamin content carefully. See that they are all there in good proportions; and be especially certain that the food contains properly high levels of vitamins A and D, two of the most perishable and important ones. Note the B-complex level, but however, a change will almost invariably give you (and your Jack Russell) some trouble.

WHEN SUPPLEMENTS ARE NEEDED

Now what about supplements of various kinds, mineral and vitamin, or the various oils? They are all okay to add to your Jack Russell's food. However, if you are feeding your Jack Russell a correct diet, and this is easy to do, no supplements are necessary unless your Jack Russell has been improperly fed, has been sick, or is having puppies. Vitamins and minerals are naturally present in all the foods; and to ensure against any loss through processing, they are added in concentrated form to the dog food you use. Except on the advice of your veterinarian, added amounts of vitamins can prove harmful to your Jack Russell! The same risk goes with minerals.

FEEDING SCHEDULE

When and how much food to give your Jack Russell? As to when (except in the instance of puppies), suit yourself. You may feed two meals per day or the same amount in one single feeding, either morning or night. As to how to prepare the food and how much to give, it is generally best to follow the directions on the food package. Your own Jack Russell may want a little more or a little less.

Fresh, cool water should always be available to your Jack Russell. This is important to good health throughout his lifetime.

ALL JACK RUSSELLS NEED TO CHEW

Puppies and young Jack Russells need something with resistance to chew on while their teeth and jaws are developing—for cutting the puppy teeth, to induce growth of the permanent teeth under the puppy teeth, to assist in getting rid of the puppy teeth at the proper time, to help the permanent teeth through the gums, to ensure normal jaw development, and to settle the permanent teeth solidly in the jaws.

The adult Jack Russell's desire to chew stems from the instinct for tooth cleaning, gum massage, and jaw exercise—plus the need for an outlet for periodic doggie tensions.

This is why dogs, especially puppies and young dogs, will often destroy property worth hundreds of dollars when their chewing instinct is not diverted from their owner's possessions. And this is why you should provide your Jack Russell with something to chew—something that has the necessary functional qualities, is desirable from the Jack Russell's viewpoint, and is safe for him.

It is very important that your Jack Russell not be permitted to chew on anything he can break or on any indigestible thing from which he can bite sizable chunks. Sharp pieces, such as from a bone which can be broken by a dog, may pierce the intestinal wall and kill. Indigestible things that can be bitten off in chunks, such as from shoes or rubber or plastic toys, may cause an intestinal

Nylafloss® is not a toy but rather a most effective agent in removing destructive plaque between teeth and beneath the gumline. Nylafloss® is safe because it is made with tough nylon strands not cotton, which is organic and will rot.

stoppage (if not regurgitated) and bring painful death, unless surgery is promptly performed.

Strong natural bones, such as 4- to 8-inch lengths of round shin bone from mature beef—either the kind you can get from a butcher or one of the variety available commercially in pet stores—may serve your Jack Russell's teething needs if his mouth is large enough to handle them effectively. You may be tempted to give your Jack Russell puppy a smaller bone and he may not be able to break it when you do, but puppies grow rapidly and the power of their jaws constantly increases until maturity. This means that a growing Jack Russell may break one of the smaller bones at any time, swallow the pieces, and die painfully before you realize what is wrong.

All hard natural bones are very abrasive. If your Jack Russell is an avid chewer, natural bones may wear away his teeth prematurely; hence, they then should be taken away from your dog when the teething purposes have been served. The badly worn, and usually painful, teeth of many mature dogs can be traced to excessive chewing on natural bones.

Contrary to popular belief, knuckle bones that can be

The Gumabone® Frisbee®* is a durable, safe flying disc with a bone molded on its top for easy retrieval from flat surfaces. Jack Russells love them! *The trademark Frisbee® is used under license by Mattel Inc., California, USA.

Roarhide® by Nylabone® is a very safe rawhide product for your JR. It is melted, molded rawhide shaped like a dog bone with 86.2% protein and no preservatives. It is naturally appealing to dogs and completely edible.

chewed up and swallowed by your Jack Russell provide little, if any, usable calcium or other nutriment. They do, however, disturb the digestion of most dogs and cause them to vomit the nourishing food they need.

Dried rawhide products of various types, shapes, sizes, and prices are available on the market and have become quite popular. However, they don't serve the primary chewing functions very well; they are a bit messy when wet from mouthing, and most Jack Russells chew them up rather rapidly—but they have been considered safe for dogs until recently. Now, more and more incidents of death, and near death, by strangulation have been reported to be the results of partially swallowed chunks of rawhide swelling in the throat. More recently, some veterinarians have been attributing cases of

acute constipation to large pieces of incompletely digested rawhide in the intestine.

A new product, molded rawhide, is very safe. During the process, the rawhide is melted and then injection molded into the familiar dog shape. It is very hard and is eagerly accepted by Jack Russells. The melting

Nylabone® products not only keep your JR's teeth clean but also provide an excellent source of entertainment and relief of doggie tensions.

Gumabones® are good for puppies because of their softer composition. These chew toys come in a variety of colors and sizes, and Jack Russells love to chew them.

process also sterilizes the rawhide. Don't confuse this with pressed rawhide, which is nothing more than small strips of rawhide squeezed together.

The nylon bones, especially those with natural meat and bone fractions added, are probably the most complete, safe, and economical answer to the chewing need. Dogs cannot break them or bite off sizable chunks; hence, they are completely safe—and being longer lasting than other things offered for the purpose, they are economical.

Hard chewing raises little bristle-like projections on the surface of the nylon bones—to provide effective interim tooth cleaning and vigorous gum massage, much in the same way your toothbrush does it for you. The little projections are raked off and swallowed in the form of thin shavings, but the chemistry of the nylon is such that they break down in the stomach fluids and pass through without effect.

The toughness of the nylon provides the strong chewing resistance needed for important jaw exercise and effectively aids teething functions, but there is no tooth wear because nylon is non-abrasive. Being inert, nylon does not support the growth of microorganisms; and it can be

Jack Russell Terriers are very protective of the toys that they own—especially their Nylafloss®!

washed in soap and water or it can be sterilized by boiling or in an autoclave.

Nylabone® is highly recommended by veterinarians as a safe, healthy nylon bone that can't splinter or chip. Nylabone® is frizzled by the dog's chewing action, creating a toothbrush-like surface that cleanses the teeth and massages the gums. Nylabone®, the only chew products made of flavor-impregnated solid nylon, are available in your local pet shop. Nylabone® is superior to the cheaper bones because it is made of virgin nylon, which is the strongest and longest-lasting type of nylon available. The cheaper bones are made from recycled or re-ground nylon scraps, and have a tendency to break apart and split easily.

Nothing, however, substitutes for periodic professional attention for your Jack Russell's teeth and gums, not any more than your toothbrush can do that for you. Have your Jack Russell's teeth cleaned at least once a year by your veterinarian (twice a year is better) and he will be happier, healthier, and far more pleasant to live with.

There are all sorts of Nylabone® products that you can buy to help keep your puppy healthy and entertained. Nylafloss®, Nylarings®, Nylaballs®, and Gumabones® are all safe, fun, and long-lasting toys.

TRAINING YOUR JACK RUSSELL

You owe proper training to your Jack Russell. The right and privilege of being trained is his birthright; and whether your Jack Russell is going to be a handsome, well-mannered housedog and companion, a show dog, or whatever possible use he may be put to, the basic training is always the same— all must start with basic obedience, or what might be called "manner training."

Your Jack Russell must come instantly when called and obey the "Sit" or "Down" command just as fast; he must walk quietly at "Heel," whether on or off lead. He must be mannerly and polite wherever he goes; he must be polite to strangers on the street and in stores. He must be mannerly in the presence of other dogs. He must not bark at children on roller skates, motorcycles, or other domestic animals. And he must be restrained from chasing cats. It is not a dog's inalienable right to chase cats, and he must be reprimanded for it.

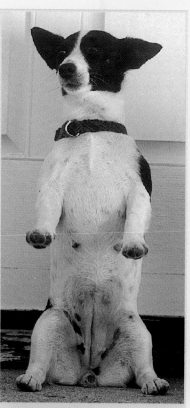

You don't have to limit your training to basic commands— teach your intelligent JR some fun tricks too!

PROFESSIONAL TRAINING

How do you go about this training? Well, it's a very simple procedure, pretty well standardized by now. First, if you can afford the extra expense, you may send your Jack Russell to a professional trainer, where in 30 to 60 days he will learn how to be a "good dog." If you enlist the services of a good professional trainer, follow his advice of when to come to see the dog. No, he won't forget you, but too-frequent visits at the wrong time may slow down his training progress. And using a "pro" trainer means that you will have to go for some training, too, after the trainer feels your Jack Russell is ready to go home. You will have to learn how your Jack Russell works, just what to expect of him and how to use what the dog has learned after he is home.

OBEDIENCE TRAINING CLASS

Another way to train your Jack Russell (many experienced Jack Russell people think this is the

It is important to teach your Jack Russell Terrier to let you know when he has to come in or go out, so you don't have to wait for him to be finished or clean up a mess.

Your Jack Russell should become used to a collar as soon as possible. Because the JR is a small dog, a thin choke-chain collar can be used.

best) is to join an obedience training class right in your own community. There is such a group in nearly every community nowadays. Here you will be working with a group of people who are also just starting out. You will actually be training your own dog, since all work is done under the direction of a head trainer who will make suggestions to you and also tell you when and how to correct your Jack Russell's errors. Then, too, working with such a group, your Jack Russell will learn to get along with other dogs. And, what is more important, he will learn to do exactly what he is told to do, no matter how much confusion there

Jack Russell Terriers are fast runners and high jumpers, and with proper training, you can enter your JR into agility competitions.

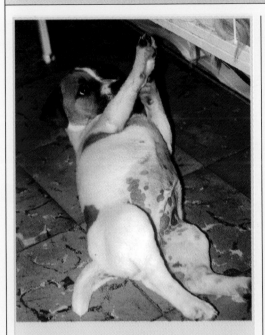

Jack Russell puppies can be very playful. They should be supervised at all times to avoid any accidents.

is around him or how great the temptation is to go his own way.

Write to your national kennel club for the location of a training club or class in your locality. Sign up. Go to it regularly—every session! Go early and leave late! Both you and your Jack Russell will benefit tremendously.

TRAIN HIM BY THE BOOK

The third way of training your Jack Russell is by the book. Yes, you can do it this way and do a good job of it too. But in using the book method, select a book, buy it, study it carefully; then study it some more, until the procedures are almost second nature to you. Then start your training. But stay with the book and its advice and exercises. Don't start in and then make up a

few rules of your own. If you don't follow the book, you'll get into jams you can't get out of by yourself. If after a few hours of short training sessions your Jack Russell is still not working as he should, get back to the book for a study session, because it's your fault, not the dog's! The procedures of dog training have been so well systemized that it must be your fault, since literally thousands of fine Jack Russells have been trained by the book.

After your Jack Russell is "letter perfect" under all conditions, then, if you wish, go on to advanced training and trick work.

Your Jack Russell will love his obedience training, and you'll burst with pride at the finished product! Your Jack Russell will enjoy life even more, and you'll enjoy your Jack Russell more. And remember—you *owe good training to your Jack Russell.*

Successful Dog Training **is one of the better dog training books on the market. It is written by Hollywood dog trainer Michael Kamer, who trains dogs for movie stars.**

Derby of Fox Run is a well-trained Jack Russell Terrier. Owner, Sandra Ferber.

Study it until you know it by heart. Having done this, and while your puppy is at home (where he should be) growing into a normal, healthy Jack Russell, go to every dog show you can possibly reach. Sit at the ringside and watch Jack Russell judging. Keep your ears and eyes open. Do your own judging, holding each of those dogs against the standard, which you now know by heart.

In your evaluations, don't start looking for faults. Look for the virtues—the best qualities. How does a given Jack Russell shape up against the standard? Having looked for and noted the virtues, then note the faults and see what prevents a given Jack Russell from standing correctly or moving well. Weigh these faults against the virtues, since, ideally, every feature of the dog should contribute to the harmonious whole dog.

"RINGSIDE JUDGING"

It's a good practice to make notes on each Jack Russell, always holding the dog against the standard. In "ringside judging," forget your personal preference for this or that feature. What does the standard say about it? Watch carefully as the judge places the dogs in a given class. It is difficult from the ringside always to see why number one was placed over the second dog. Try to follow the judge's reasoning. Later try to talk with the judge after he is finished. Ask him questions as to why he placed certain Jack Russells and not others. Listen while the judge explains his placings, and, I'll say right here, any judge worthy of his license should be able to give reasons.

When you're not at the ringside, talk with the fanciers and breeders who have Jack Russells.

The hurdle race is a popular event at terrier trials. Jack Russells excel at the race because they are fast and agile dogs.

The Jack Russell Terrier proves himself in many areas of competition, for he is highly trainable and enjoys the spotlight.

Don't be afraid to ask opinions or say that you don't know. You have a lot of listening to do, and it will help you a great deal and speed up your personal progress if you are a good listener.

THE NATIONAL CLUB

You will find it worthwhile to join the national Jack Russell club and to subscribe to its magazine. From the national club, you will learn the location of an approved regional club near you. Now, when your young Jack Russell is eight to ten months old, find out the dates of match shows in your section of the country. These differ from regular shows only in that no championship points are given. These shows are especially designed to launch young dogs (and new handlers) on a show career.

ENTER MATCH SHOWS

With the ring deportment you have watched at big shows firmly in mind and practice, enter your Jack Russell in as many match shows as you can. When in the ring, you have two jobs. One is to see to it that your Jack Russell is always being seen to its best advantage. The other job is to keep your eye on the judge to see what he may want you to do next. Watch only the judge and your Jack Russell. Be quick and be alert; do exactly as the judge directs. Don't speak to him except to answer his questions. If he does something you don't like, don't say so. And don't irritate the judge (and everybody else) by constantly talking and fussing with your dog.

In moving about the ring, remember to keep clear of dogs beside you or in front of you. It is my advice to you *not* to show your Jack Russell in a regular point show until he is at least close to maturity and after both you and your dog have had time to perfect ring manners and poise in the match shows.

The highest JRTCA awards go to field and work trial winners, not to dogs groomed to show well as a matter of form.

YOUR JACK RUSSELL'S HEALTH

Fortunately, because the JR is a natural and unspoiled breed, it has relatively few health problems that are common to the breed. Those illnesses most often seen in the JR are usually associated with its function as a hunting dog.

MANGE

If you hunt with your JR, he is apt to contract mange, which is commonly found on foxes and rats. Suspect mange if you see scales and oozing patches on your dog's skin. The condition is caused by a mite that burrows under the skin. Soon your dog will be so uncomfortable that he will begin to scratch and bite, often pulling out large patches of coat. There are two types of mange: red and sarcoptic. The latter, characterized by itchy scabs, is more common, particularly if you hunt your dog or enter it into quarry.

Red mange is more common in puppies and older dogs. Though both types of mange are treatable, red mange sometimes goes away by itself. Sarcoptic mange is contagious to other animals and humans and requires immediate treatment. Don't attempt to treat either type of mange with home remedies. If you suspect the condition is present, consult your veterinarian.

EAR CANKER

Ear canker is caused by the otodetic mite, a parasite that thrives in your dog's outer ear. This mite causes so much discomfort that your dog will often scratch until its ear begins to bleed and a secondary infection develops. Suspect ear canker if you notice a brownish, smelly substance emanating from your JR's ear. The condition requires immediate treatment, so get your dog to the vet as soon as possible. As a hunting dog, your JR is likely to pick up ear canker at some time, so it's best to check the ears daily and keep them clean. There are a number of antiseptic ear cleaners sold over-the-counter that will do the job.

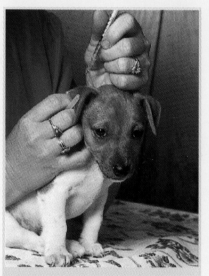

Immunization shots for canine diseases such as rabies, distemper, and hepatitis should be given to your JR for the first time at six weeks of age.

LYME DISEASE

Another disease that could strike your JR is Lyme disease. Even if you don't hunt or quarry the dog, it's likely that you will spend ample time walking in parks, woods or near lakes with your JR. All of these settings are laden with the small deer tick that carries Lyme disease. The disease was first isolated in the town from whence it gets its name — Lyme, Connecticut. The disease itself is serious and can affect both you and your pet. It is transmitted by a bite from a carrier tick and is characterized by swelling around the joint area. In humans, the condition can be mistaken for other ailments, especially viruses or the flu. If you find a dear tick on your dog, or suspect you've been bitten by one, call your vet or a Lyme disease hotline.

Although there is no equivalent human vaccination currently available, your JR can be immunized against Lyme disease and given a yearly booster to prevent it.

IMMUNIZATION

As with all pets, your JR needs to be immunized against the most common canine diseases: rabies, distemper, leptospirosis, coronavirus, parvovirus, hepatitis and parainfluenza. The breeder should give the pups their first shots in early puppyhood, usually at the six-week mark. Once you get your puppy, it should begin its series of puppy shots at regular intervals as suggested by your veterinarian. Thereafter, the dog needs to be re-vaccinated every year.

BORDETELLA

If you kennel your JR, you should have it immunized against bordetella, which is also called "kennel cough." Bordetella is a bacterial infection with symptoms that range from running nose and eyes to the characteristic hacking cough. Once an animal is infected, the disease can spread through a whole kennel like wild fire.

PARASITES

The JR is more likely to be infected with parasites than many other breeds because of its sporting nature and the time it spends outdoors. Fleas and ticks are the most common pests. If you hunt or quarry your dog, it is likely he will pick up one or both of these parasites at one time or another. Because the flea and tick feed on your pet's blood supply, anemia can result if your JR becomes infested. If your dog ingests a flea, it can also contract tapeworm, which, if not treated, can lead to anemia. Sporting breeds like the JR should be treated regularly with flea dips and shampoos. Some owners find flea and tick collars useful.

It's absolutely essential to keep your pet's living quarters clean to prevent flea infestation. A female flea lays hundreds of eggs that hatch and become adults, which continue the process of multiplying within three weeks time. Carpets and cracks in floors or concrete are perfect breeding grounds. That's why it's so essential to effectively treat the entire home or kennel regularly to keep it flea-free. Besides the over-the-counter flea products and foggers available, there are several non-toxic products on the market with a boraxo base that can be brushed into the carpet. Ask your vet for suggestions about how to treat your pet's environment.

Anytime your JR comes back from a romp in the woods or fields, always check him for ticks, which commonly burrow into the dogs skin around the neck, ears or limbs. If you discover a tick, you can remove it yourself with a pair of tweezers. First dab the spot with alcohol, then grab the tick with the tweezers as close to the point of attachment as possible and pull it out. Flush the tick down the toilet and dab the dog's skin with antiseptic. Be sure you have completely removed all of the tick from your pet's skin or infection can result.

In the course of your JR's outdoor travels, he can also contract various internal parasites like hookworms, roundworms, tapeworms and whipworms.

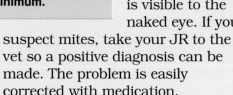

Fleas can be an itchy nuisance to your Jack Russell. Treat him regularly with flea dips and shampoos to keep infestations to a minimum.

Suspect worm infestation if your dog's coat becomes lackluster and its abdomen distended. A stool sample taken to your vet will determine if worms are present. If so, your vet will prescribe the correct medication to rid the dog of the parasite. Do not attempt to worm the dog yourself. Never routinely worm a healthy dog. Let your vet make the diagnosis.

Although coccidia and giardia are more commonly found in puppies, your JR is susceptible if he goes near lakes or ponds where beaver or other wildlife may be present. Symptoms include loss of weight, dull coat and watery diarrhea. Your vet can make a positive diagnosis by examining a fresh stool sample.

If you actively hunt or quarry your JR, he should be checked for these common parasites routinely, preferably every few months.

EAR MITES

If your JR suddenly starts scratching his ears with his paws or rubbing them against the ground and shaking his head, the dog could have ear mites. If you have more than one pet, ear mites can be spread from one to the other. Symptoms include a waxy, foul-smelling, dark discharge in the ear canal that is visible to the naked eye. If you

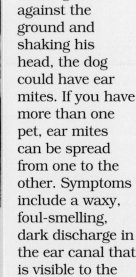

suspect mites, take your JR to the vet so a positive diagnosis can be made. The problem is easily corrected with medication.

HEARING IMPAIRMENT

Though it does not occur with enough frequency to be characterized as a common problem in the breed, hearing impairment is occasionally found in the JR. If you suspect that your dog isn't responding to your voice properly, it's a good idea to have its hearing tested by your vet.